AF252158

New Mexican Chiles

Additional Terra Nova Books in
The Pepper Pantry Series by Dave DeWitt:
The Essential Chile Sauce Guide
The Essential Hot Spice Guide
Jalapeños
Ancho and Poblano Chiles
Sweet Heat

THE PEPPER PANTRY

New Mexican Chiles

Dave DeWitt, *the Pope of Peppers*

Terra Nova Books

SANTA FE, NEW MEXICO

Library of Congress Control Number 2018934833

Distributed by SCB Distributors, (800) 729-6423

New Mexican Chiles. Copyright © 2012 by Dave DeWitt
All rights reserved
Second edition published 2018 by Terra Nova Books
Printed in the United States of America

No part of this book may be used, reproduced or transmitted in any form by any means, electronic or mechanical, including photocopying, recording, or by any information storage and retrieval system, without express permission in writing from the publisher except in the case of brief quotations embedded in critical articles and reviews. Send inquiries to Terra Nova Books, 33 Alondra Road, Santa Fe, New Mexico 87508.

Published by Terra Nova Books, Santa Fe, New Mexico.
www.TerraNovaBooks.com

ISBN 978-1-938288-28-9

Contents

Introduction

According to many accounts, chile peppers were introduced into what is now the U.S. from Mexico by Capitán General Juan de Oñate, the founder of Santa Fe, in 1598. However, they may have been introduced to the Pueblo Indians of New Mexico by the Antonio Espejo expedition of 1582–83. According to one member of the expedition, Baltasar Obregón, "They have no chile, but the natives were given some seed to plant." By 1601, chiles were on the list of Indian crops, according to colonist Francisco de Valverde, who also complained that mice were a pest that ate chile pods off the plants in the field.

"A la primera cocinera se le va un chile entero," goes one old Spanish *dicho,* or saying: "To the best lady cook goes the whole chile." And so it is that the chile pepper is the single most important food brought from Mexico that defines New

Mexican cuisine. After the Spanish began settlement, the cultivation of chile peppers exploded, and soon, they were grown all over New Mexico. It is likely that many varieties were cultivated, including early forms of jalapeños, serranos, poblanos, and pasillas. But one variety that adapted particularly well to New Mexico was a long green chile that turned red in the fall. Formerly called "Anaheim" because of its transfer to more-settled California around 1900, the New Mexican chiles were cultivated for hundreds of years in the region with such dedication that several distinct varieties developed.

These varieties, or "landraces," called "Chimayó" and "Española," had adapted to particular environments and are still planted in the fields they were grown in centuries ago; they constitute a small but distinct part of the tons of pods produced each year in New Mexico.

In 1846, William Emory, chief engineer of the U.S. Army's Topographic Unit, was surveying the New Mexico landscape and its customs. He described this meal eaten in Bernalillo, just north of Albuquerque: "Roast chicken, stuffed with onions; then mutton, boiled with onions; then followed various other dishes, all dressed with the everlasting onion; and the whole terminated by chile, the glory of New Mexico."

Emory went on to relate his experience: "Chile the Mexicans consider the chef-d'oeuvre of the cuisine, and seem really to revel in it; but the first mouthful brought the tears trickling down my cheeks, very much to the amusement of the spectators with their leather-lined throats. It was red pepper, stuffed with minced meat."

PART 1

"Anaheim"
and All
the Rest of
Them

NOMENCLATURE

For nearly a century, confusion has reigned over the proper name for the long green varieties of chile that turn red in the fall. Originally, they were developed and grown in New Mexico; however, seeds were transported to California during the early part of the twentieth century, and the pod type was given the name "Anaheim."

Since few if any chiles are grown near Anaheim these days, it makes little sense to use that name for them. Recently, chile experts at New Mexico State University have decided on a more-accurate descriptive term. In future, the name of this pod type will be "New Mexican." Varieties within this type will include "Anaheims," California strains, as well as the numerous New Mexico-grown varieties such as "NuMex Big Jim" and "NuMex 6-4." To put it simply, Anaheim has been reduced from a pod type to a variety, and the pod type has been renamed New Mexican.

CHILE HISTORY

The earliest cultivated chiles in New Mexico were smaller than those of today; indeed, they were (and still are, in some cases) considered a spice. But as the landraces developed and the size of the pods increased, the food value of chiles became evident. There was just one problem: The bewildering sizes and shapes of the chile peppers made it very difficult for farmers to determine which variety of chile they were growing from year to year. And there was no way to tell how large the pods might be, or how hot. The demand for chiles was increasing as the population of the state did, so it was time for modern horticulture to take over.

In 1907, Fabián García, a horticulturist at the Agricultural Experiment Station at the College of Agriculture and Mechanical Arts (now New Mexico State University), began his first experiments in breeding more-standardized chile varieties, and, in 1908, he published "Chile Culture," the first chile bulletin from the Agricultural Experiment Station. In 1913, García became director of the Experiment Station and expanded his breeding program.

Finally, in 1917, after ten years of experimenting with various strains of pasilla chiles, he released New Mexico No. 9, the first attempt to grow chiles with a dependable pod size and heat level. The No. 9 variety became the chile standard in New Mexico until 1950, when Roy Harper, another horticulturist, released New Mexico No. 6, a variety that matured earlier, produced higher yields, and was wilt resistant and less pungent than No. 9.

The New Mexico No. 6 variety was by far the biggest breakthrough in the chile breeding program. According to the late Dr. Roy Nakayama, who succeeded Harper as director of the New Mexico Agricultural Experiment Station, "The No. 6 variety changed the image of chile from a ball of fire that sent consumers rushing to the water jug to that of a multipurpose vegetable with a pleasing flavor. Commercial production and marketing, especially of green chiles and sauces, have been growing steadily since people around the world have discovered the delicious taste of chile without the overpowering pungency."

In 1957, the New Mexico No. 6 variety was modified and made less pungent again, and the new variety was called "New Mexico No. 6-4." The No. 6-4 variety became the chile industry standard in New Mexico, and more than fifty-five years later, is still the most popular chile commercially grown in the state.

Today, Dr. Paul Bosland, who took over the chile breeding program from Nakayama, is developing new varieties that are more resistant to chile wilt, a fungal disease that can devastate fields. He has also created varieties to produce brown, orange, and yellow ristras for the home decoration market. The breeding and development of new chile varieties—in addition to research into wild species, post-harvest packaging, and genetics—is an ongoing, major project at New Mexico State. Bosland has introduced new versions of New Mexico classics, including "NuMex 6-4 Heritage" and "NuMex Big Jim Heritage." New Mexico is one of the largest commercial producers of chile peppers in the United States, with about ten thousand acres under cultivation.

VARIETIES

The most important varieties of the New Mexican pod type are: "Anaheim M" (mild, eight-inch pods); "Chimayó" (a landrace from northern New Mexico with thin-walled, six-inch pods); "Española Improved" (pods five to six inches, medium heat); "Fresno" (erect two-inch pods, medium heat); "NuMex 6-4 Heritage" (the most common New Mexican variety, pods are seven inches long with medium heat); "NuMex Big Jim Heritage" (pods up to twelve inches, medium heat); "NuMex Eclipse" (chocolate-brown, mild, five-inch pods); "NuMex Joe E. Parker" (improved 6-4 variety); "NuMex Sunrise" (bright yellow, mild, five-inch pods); "NuMex Sunset" (orange, mild, five-inch pods); "NuMex R Naky" (pods five to seven inches long with mild heat); and "NuMex Sandia" (medium hot, six-inch pods with thin walls).

For the recipes awaiting you in these pages, it's chef's choice as to which New Mexican chile to use. But whatever type you pick, there's one fact you can have confidence in: They're all delicious.

HEAT SCALE

New Mexican varieties vary between 100 and 2,500 Scoville Heat Units. Generally speaking, New Mexico-grown chiles are hotter than those cultivated in California.

PART 2

From Seed
to Shelf

Botanical Description

Since there are significant differences among New Mexican varieties, what follows is a description of the most commonly grown variety, "NuMex 6–4 Heritage." The plant measures twenty to thirty inches high, and has an intermediate number of stems and a habit varying between prostrate and compact. Corolla color is white with no spots. The leaves are ovate, medium green, fairly smooth, and approximately three inches long and two inches wide. The flower corollas are white with no spots. The fruit is smooth, elongated, pendant, measuring six to seven inches, and bluntly pointed. It is dark green, maturing to various shades of red. Some ornamentals are yellow or brown.

Cultivation and Preservation

Hundreds of articles and at least two books—*The Pepper Garden* and *The Complete Chile Pepper Book*—have been written on the home and commercial cultivation of the Capsicums, so there's far too much information to go into great detail in this section. Instead, it is designed as a basic gardening guide for beginners using organic techniques.

The Strategy

The combination of long growing times of the increasingly popular exotic chile varieties and the medium to short growing seasons in many parts of North America forces many gardeners to examine their strategy. To get the maximum number of peppers from these potentially prolific varieties, the plants need enough time to produce and ripen the pods. That often means extending the natural growing season at the front end, the back end, or both.

STARTING SEEDS

To stretch the beginning of the pepper-growing season, start the plants indoors around January if the garden is in the North, February in the South. Plant the pepper seeds in "recycled" plastic six packs (from plants bought at nurseries) filled with a loose seed-starting mix. Plant far more seeds than the number of plants needed for the garden, thinning out the weakest plants later, and perhaps even planting a few extra seedlings in pots that can be moved indoors come fall.

After sowing the seeds in the premoistened seed-starting mix, set the six packs (or seed-starting flat or pots or whatever) on a source of bottom heat (such as a heating cable, a seed-starting mat, or the top of a refrigerator) to boost germination. Cover the setup loosely with plastic to retain moisture, spritz the surface lightly with tepid water every day if it seems dry, and then, after the seeds have sprouted, remove the plastic and move the containers to where the seedlings will receive plenty of bright light: either the sill of a superbright, clean window; very close to a four-tube fluorescent fixture; or under some high intensity grow lights.

The pepper plants will grow more foliage and flowers (and therefore more fruit) if the seedlings are prevented from becoming rootbound. So either start them in large containers or transplant them into increasingly larger pots, starting when the seedlings hit the four-leaf stage. Then, when the seedlings are finally transplanted outside, their roots will be vigorous and spread-out rather than cramped, and the plants will get off to a running start.

PESTS

A couple of pests do go after pepper seedlings. Aphids especially like to attack young plants indoors. Fight these little pests by knocking them off the seedlings with a spray mixture of soapy water and chile powder. To make it, add about one half to one teaspoon of the hottest, most finely ground chile powder to a quart of ready-made insecticidal soap solution (mixed according to the label) or to a quart of water containing two drops of dishwashing soap, well mixed. As always, test the spray on one or two plants before spraying the rest of them.

The other "pest" most known for its tendency to damage pepper seedlings (and thus reduce potential yields) is a cat, who wil graze on your pepper seedlings if given the chance, so keep the six packs and seedling tray out of reach.

TRANSPLANTING

Soon, the pampered peppers will be moved from the protected sanctuary of the home or greenhouse into the brutal spring environment of high winds, low temperatures, and bright light. To toughen the seedlings' stems so they can withstand those outdoor winds, place them in front of a fan for three to seven days before they are scheduled to go outside. Keep the fan on day and night at a setting that's just high enough to create a moderate breeze. Don't blow the seedlings over, just create some good air circulation.

Then, sometime around the last frost date, begin to further prepare the seedlings for their move outdoors by "hardening them off": Place them outside for increasing periods of time each day, or even overnight if a nice warm spell hits, over a one-to-two-week period.

Preparing the Plot

While hardening off those seedlings, prepare their future garden site. They'll grow best in raised beds in most regions, and in sunken beds in dry climates. The pepper garden should ideally be located somewhere that peppers haven't grown for several years to help prevent disease problems. Admittedly, a strict crop rotation is hard to do in a small garden, but a pepper planting can at least follow a spring crop of peas. Try not to grow peppers in the same spot two years in a row.

Dig some compost or aged manure into the pepper bed before planting. This will be all the nutrition the peppers need for the growing season to come. Use aged (not fresh) manure to ensure against nitrogen overdose, which can cause low yields. There have been cases of six-foot-tall jalapeño plants with plenty of foliage but no pods because the grower fed them too much nitrogen too fast.

If you are growing peppers in the North (or anyplace where the ground is chilly), warm up the soil by covering it with black plastic for a few days before the planting.

Don't pull up this "mulch" later on; leave it right where it is, and plant the peppers into holes cut in the plastic—this will keep the soil warm, decrease the water needs, and prevent weeds.

When planting, use only the healthiest and most-vigorous seedlings. Leggy, stunted, or aphid-damaged plants will not recover enough to fulfill their yield potential. Space the seedlings about six to twelve inches apart. Many garden guidelines suggest a twelve-inch spacing between pepper plants, but smaller-podded varieties can easily be squeezed into a six-inch space.

Don't plant all the seedlings in the ground, though. Save some of the plants for growing in containers outside, so the pots can be moved indoors to a brightly lit area when the weather turns cool in fall.

The newly transplanted peppers will need as much warmth as they can get. Protect them from low temperatures by covering the plants with a floating row cover, such as Reemay. Some gardeners surround their seedlings with water-filled innertubes or Wall-o-Waters (flexible plastic tubes arranged in a circle and filled with water; they are sold at garden centers, nurseries, and by mail). The water absorbs heat from the sun during the day and then holds onto it after temperatures start to cool. Overnight, the water releases that heat, keeping the soil and air around the seedlings nice and warm. Another warm-water technique is to fill several gallon-sized plastic milk jugs with water and bury them halfway in the ground next to each seedling (being careful not to disturb the plant's roots when digging).

When summer arrives, weeds may try to seize control of the pepper patch. Prevent them at all costs. Weeds not only look ugly but also can harbor pests like leafhoppers, which spread curly top virus to pepper plants (something that happened with devastating effect throughout New Mexico in 1995). So keep those hoppers homeless by making the garden weed free.

For gardeners who live in warm zones, the summer sun can be more of a hindrance than a help for getting high yields. Intense sunlight can actually cook peppers (a problem called sunscald) and decrease the yield of usable fruits. If you are gardening in a high-altitude region with intense sunlight, cover the peppers with shade netting (available at garden centers or by mail order). Rig a makeshift frame over the peppers, and drape the shade cloth over it so the peppers remain easy to tend under their "tent." Varieties such as habaneros and rocotos are especially prone to sunscald, and both perform and yield better under the netting than in open, unshaded plots.

During the hottest days of July and August, pepper plants can lose a lot of water through their leaves. When this occurs, the leaves wilt, and the flowers (and sometimes the fruit) drop right off the plants. Reduce this water loss by boosting the humidity around the plants with a thick layer of mulch such as dried grass clippings (placed on top of any plastic mulch you may be using).

Once the plants start producing their peppers, another little trick can maximize the yields, at least with pepper varieties that are eaten green, such as jalapeños, serranos, and the New Mexican varieties. Increase the total yield of these varieties by continually picking the peppers when they reach their largest "mature green" size, and not waiting for them to fully ripen on the plant. A pepper plant that reaches its "fruit load" (the maximum weight of peppers it can support) will stop flowering and fruiting even though a month or more may be left in the growing season. Removing the mature green fruits signals the plant to continue flowering and setting fruit throughout the remainder of the season, and the result is more pods per plant..

Harvest Time

Often, the first frost of the year does not signal the end of the growing season. The early frost may be followed by an "Indian summer" that brings enough warm weather to keep peppers growing for another three or four weeks. But to use this extended season, it is necessary to cover the plants. There are many good crop protectors: cotton bed sheets, clear or black plastic, nylon netting, plastic row covers, even large cardboard boxes placed over individual plants. The material should be thick and dense enough to retain ground heat but not so thick that it will break off branches if it gets weighted down by rain or snow.

Place the covers in position as early in the day as possible, say between 4 and 6 p.m., on the evening of the frost so there's still some heat to retain. (It gets cool fast at night in the fall.) And be sure to remove the covers as soon as it's warm enough the following day.

If the temperature is going to drop below 28 degrees, though, the covering efforts will probably not be enough to protect the plants from the cold. But there are your other plants, those peppers that have been growing in pots. Move them indoors before the first frost, and the plants will over-winter nicely. If you don't have any peppers in pots, dig up a few of the healthiest favorites in the garden (but don't dig up a struggler hoping it'll recover inside, because it won't), pot them in a soil that drains well, and move them inside. These plants may drop most of their leaves over the winter, but most will survive and come back strong, especially if they are pruned in the spring, cutting off any branches that look dead and brown rather than green. The plants will sprout new growth vigorously after such a pruning, even if you cut them back severely.

Gardeners can even make this indoor overwintering and spring pruning a perennial event, because peppers are perennials when grown in frost-free conditions. Wintered-over pepper plants need regular watering, but unless you are actively growing them by providing artificial light, there is no need to fertilize them until they resume growing in the spring.

ROASTING AND PEELING THE PODS

The New Mexican varieties have tough skins that are usually blistered and peeled before being used in recipes that require cooking. Blistering or roasting the chiles is the process of heating the fresh pods to the point that the transparent skin is separated from the meat of the chile so it can be removed.

To roast and peel pepper pods, first cut a small slit in the pod close to the stem end so the steam can escape. The pods can be placed on a baking sheet and put directly under the broiler, or on a screen on top of the burner. They can also be plunged into hot cooking oil to loosen the skins, but that method is messy and not recommended.

The easiest way is to use a barbecue grill. Place the pods on a grill about five to six inches from the coals or gas flames, turning them often. Blisters will soon form, indicating that the skin is separating, but take care that the pods are blistered all over, or they will not peel properly. Although the pods may burn slightly, be careful they do not blacken entirely, or they will be overcooked and nearly impossible to peel. The idea is to use intense heat for short periods of time rather than low heat for a long time. During the charcoal roasting process, the sugar and starch caramelize in the chile, which imparts a "cooked" flavor, while a rapid roasting over high heat leaves the chile tasting more "raw."

And during the roasting process, why not save a few perfectly formed pods and make a classic dish of chiles rellenos—stuffed peppers? Remove the pods from the grill with tongs, wrap them in damp paper towels immediately, and place them in a plastic bag to steam for ten to fifteen minutes. For a crisper, less-cooked pepper, plunge the pods in ice water to stop the cooking process.

Chile roasters have become common in the Southwest, and these cylindrical cages with gas jets below can roast a forty-pound sack of chile in a lot less time than it takes to roast pods on the grill. Although this is a more-convenient way to process large quantities of pods, there are some drawbacks. Occasionally, the pods are roasted unevenly, leaving some difficult to peel. The pods are usually placed in a large plastic bag to steam after being roasted, and must be processed as soon as they have cooled enough to handle. If allowed to sit for too long, bacterial growth can cause the pods to spoil.

After the chiles have cooled down, it's time for the final step. If you've done a good job of roasting them, peeling your chiles is fast and easy. Simply start at either end, and pull off the skin, wearing gloves, of course. We generally pull from the tip back toward the stem, but it depends on the roasting job. Occasionally, you will run into problems with deep indentations, or "valleys," on the pod; blistering those "valleys" is difficult without burning the surrounding areas. In these cases, you simply have to go in with a knife and scrape off any remaining skin.

Because the hotter varieties of green chile have thinner flesh than the mild ones, it is difficult to peel them and come up with an intact pod; they tend to tear and split apart during the peeling process. If you are going to chop the chile before using, it really doesn't matter if the pods split. If you want chiles to stuff, however, this can be a disaster. To produce roasted and peeled green chile pods that are intact, simply start with mild chile pods, which have much-thicker flesh.

At this point, most people like to cut off the stem and remove the seeds. The easiest way is to simply cut off the very top of the chile along with the stem, and then scrape the seeds out the open end. If you really want to reduce the firepower, you can also remove the veins (the placental tissue) that run the length of the pod and attach the seeds to the pod). You've now completed the whole process and have a chile pod that is ready to eat, cook with, or freeze.

PRESERVING THE CROP

Freezing chiles is an excellent way of preserving them. Chiles that have been frozen retain all the characteristics of fresh chiles except for their texture. Since the individual cell walls are ruptured by the freezing of the water within each cell, the chiles lose their crisp texture.

Another result of the freezing process is to spread the capsaicin throughout the chile. This occurs with the rupturing of the cell walls, and can make some chiles seem hotter after freezing than they were beforehand. However, research indicates that freezing chiles does not actually make them hotter. There is simply nothing the freezing process can do, either physically or chemically, to increase the heat of a chile.

There are different requirements for freezing chiles, depending on their size. Large chiles may be frozen at any stage once they have been roasted. That is, they may be frozen before peeling (freezing actually makes them easier to peel) or after peeling and deseeding. They may be frozen whole or chopped.

The easiest way to freeze large chiles is to put them into freezer bags, double-bag them, and place them in the freezer. You can also wrap them in heavy foil or freezer wrap, or you can pack them in rigid plastic containers. A handy way to freeze chopped New Mexico green chile is in plastic ice cube trays. After the trays are frozen, the chile cubes can be popped out and stored in bags. Then they can be used when making soups, stews, or other recipes without having to pry apart blocks of frozen chiles.

Fresh red chile paste or sauce can be stored in plastic containers or zip bags and frozen to use all year long. The paste holds up well in the freezer and really helps to cut meal preparation time.

DRYING CHILES

The oldest, easiest, and most common way to preserve chiles is to dry them. Aside from a few thick-walled, meaty varieties such as jalapeños, most chiles are well-preserved by drying them at home. There are several ways to dry chiles, using both traditional methods and new technologies.

MAKING RISTRAS

The ristra, or chile string, is the oldest and also the most attractive method, and there are several ways of assembling the strings. Traditional ristras are made by tying New Mexico red chiles together with cotton string, in clusters of three. Start by wrapping the string around the three stems a couple of times, then bring it up between two of the chiles, and finish off with a half-hitch over the stems. Continue using the same piece of string, tying up groups of three chiles until the ristra gets too awkward to handle. Then just cut the string and start again. Making a thirty-six-inch ristra requires around fifteen pounds of fresh red pods.

When all the chiles have been strung by threes, they then get braided onto a length of strong twine or wire. Hanging the twine from an overhead support greatly simplifies this stage of the assembly. Braid the chiles from the bottom of the twine as if braiding hair, using the twine as one braid and chiles from each grouping as the other two. Be sure to push each group down tightly against the others to ensure an attractive, full-bodied ristra.

These days, some ristra makers have resorted to "tying" the groups of three chiles with rubber bands, then slipping each group over a wire to form the ristra. This is considerably faster than the traditional method, but the ristras tend to be a bit skinny, and last only as long as the rubber bands hold out.

One final way to make a ristra is to use a large needle threaded with string. Push the needle through the bottom of the stem where it widens out, pressing the chiles up tightly against each other. Again, this tends to produce thin-looking ristras, but the problem can be overcome by hanging several strings together. It is also a handy way to handle smaller chiles such as cayennes or piquins, which require a lot of time and dexterity to string in the traditional way.

Unless you live in an arid climate, it is important to dry your ristras someplace where the air circulates freely. If they are hung in a home in a damp climate, there is a good chance some of the chiles will rot. Being hung from a tree or in an open porch should give the ristra a good chance to dry properly. If a few of the chiles do start to rot, just pull them off the string; if you've begun with a nice full ristra, you'll never miss them!

Another good reason to dry your ristra outside is that if any of the chiles start to rot, they may drip a liquid that will stain anything it touches. (After all, chiles are used to produce red coloring that is used in food products.) So you might want to reconsider before hanging your fresh ristra over your two-inch-deep, snow-white pile carpet. And one final disturbing note: Chiles that turn bad attract fruit flies by the zillions. Obviously, it makes a lot of sense to hang them outside to dry!

OTHER DRYING METHODS

Another way to dry chiles, and, in fact, nearly the only way to dry some of the thick-fleshed types, is by using a food dehydrator. As we mentioned earlier, jalapeños and several other chiles simply will not air dry. They will, however, dry well in a dehydrator. Simply place them in a single layer on the racks and follow the instructions for your model. Cutting the thick-fleshed chiles in half or into several pieces helps speed up the process.

Many people think that drying in an oven is just as effective, which unfortunately is not always the case. Dehydrators not only supply heat but also constantly circulate air through the unit. Ovens usually only supply heat, which means that meaty chiles could spoil rather than dry.

If you do use an oven, set it on the lowest possible heat. Cut the chiles in half, remove the seeds, and place them on a baking tray. Check the chiles every hour or so to make sure they are not burning. When they are brittle, they are ready.

It's possible to dry small quantities of chiles in a microwave oven after chopping them into small pieces. This takes no time at all, especially for smaller, thin-fleshed varieties. However, the method will not work for whole pods.

Roasted and peeled fresh green New Mexico chiles can also be dried, and, in fact, drying fresh green was the only way to preserve it in the days before freezers. The recipe that follows for Chile Pasado will show how. But a word of warning: Don't get upset by the appearance of the dried green, since it turns black and looks more like road-kill than anything you'd want to eat! When rehydrated, though, it plumps up, turns almost green, and is extremely tasty.

MAKING POWDERS

All dried chiles can be ground into powder—and most are, including the habanero. Crushed chiles, or those coarsely ground with some of the seeds, are called quebrado. Coarse powders are referred to as *caribe*, while the finer powders are termed *molido*. The milder powders, such as New Mexican, can also be used as the base for sauces, but the hotter powders such as cayenne and piquin are used when heat is needed more than flavor.

Adventurous cooks can experiment with creating powders of specific colors. For example, collect the different varieties of green, yellow, orange, red, and brown chiles, and separate them into their respective colors. The colors of the powders vary from a bright, electric red-orange (chiltepins) to light green (dried jalapeños) to a dark brown that verges on black (ancho). The colored powders can then be combined with spices, as in chili powder, or be stored for later use. Another use for the powders is to turn them into green, yellow, orange, red, or brown chile pastes. Since some of the colors of the powders tend to be a bit dull, they can be brightened up by adding a few drops of the appropriate food coloring when making the pastes.

In some kitchens, more powders than whole pods are available because the concentrated powders take up less space. Store them in small, airtight bottles. The fresher the powders, the better they taste, so don't grind up too many pods. Use an electric spice mill, and be sure to wear a painter's mask to protect the nose and throat from the pungent powder. Many cooks experiment by changing the powders called for in recipes.

Chile Pasado (Chile of the Past)

Here is the way green chile was preserved before the invention of canning and freezers. The method assumes that you live in a dry climate like New Mexico or Arizona. If not, remove the stems from the chile and place the pods in a food dehydrator until brittle. You also can put them in an oven set at the lowest heat possible, but you must monitor them carefully. There are about ten medium-sized pods to a pound.

2 pounds (about 20) New Mexico green chile pods
String

Roast the chile pods on a charcoal or gas grill until they blister and start to blacken, turning often. Remove them from the grill and place in a plastic bag with a wet paper towel for half an hour. Remove them and carefully peel the skin, leaving the stem and seeds intact. Tie four pods together by wrapping string around the stems, and place them over a line outside in the sun. Do not let the chiles get wet from rain, and wrap them lightly in cheesecloth to protect them from flies and other insects. Drying time varies with humidity levels, but dry them until they are very dark and brittle. To store, break off the stems and place the dried pods in a zip bag, then put it in a second zip bag. Place the bags in the freezer for optimum results, especially if you live in a humid climate. Because they are brittle, breaking off the stems will sometimes cause the pods to break into strips and other pieces.

(continued on next page)

To reconstitute the pods, put them in a pot of boiling water for one minute. Remove from the heat, and let stand for five minutes, then drain. Use them in any recipe calling for green chile in any form except whole pods.

Yield: About 3 ounces   **Heat scale:** Varies but usually medium

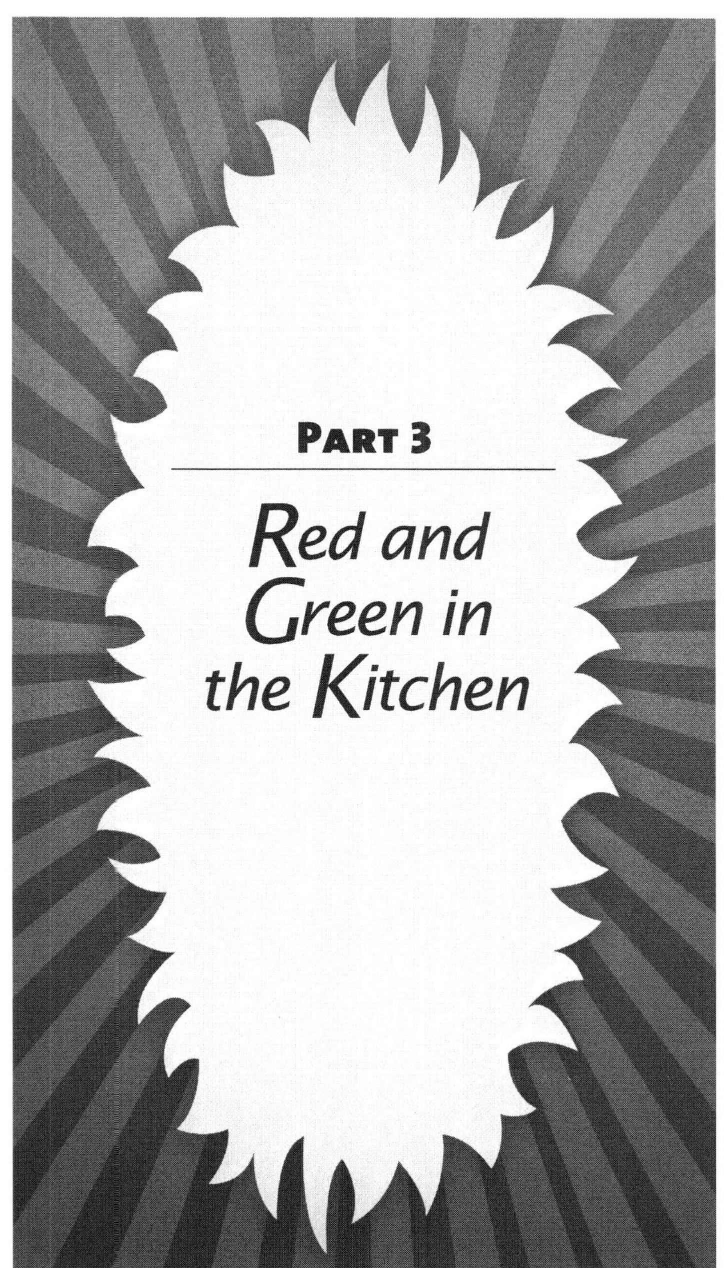

PART 3

Red and
Green in
the Kitchen

Culinary Usage

All the primary dishes in New Mexican cuisine contain chile peppers: sauces, stews, carne adovada, enchiladas, posole, tamales, huevos rancheros, and many combination vegetable dishes. The intense use of chiles as a food rather than just as a spice or condiment is what differentiates New Mexican cuisine from that of Texas or Arizona. In neighboring states, chile powders are used as a seasoning for beef or chicken broth-based "chili gravies," which are thickened with flour or cornstarch before they are added to, say, enchiladas. In New Mexico, the sauces are made from pure chiles and are thickened by reducing the mixture of the processed pods and water.

New Mexico chile sauces are cooked and pureed, while salsas use fresh ingredients and are uncooked. Debates rage over whether tomatoes should be used in cooked sauces such as red chile sauce for enchiladas. Despite the recipes in numerous cookbooks, traditional cooked red sauces do not contain tomatoes, though uncooked salsas do. New Mexicans love chile peppers so much that they have become the de facto state symbol. Houses are adorned with strings of dried ristras. Images of the pods are emblazoned on signs, T-shirts, coffee mugs, posters, windsocks, and even underwear. In the late summer and early fall, the aroma of roasting chiles fills the air all over New Mexico and produces a state of bliss for chileheads..

Sauces,
Salsas, and
Condiments

Green Chile Sauce

This versatile sauce is basic to New Mexican cuisine. It's at its best made with fresh green chile. Finely diced pork can be added, but cook the sauce an additional half-hour. Use this sauce over enchiladas, burritos, eggs for breakfast, or on chiles rellenos. It will keep for about five days in the refrigerator, and freezes well.

> 1 small onion, finely chopped
>
> 1 clove garlic, minced
>
> 2 tablespoons vegetable oil
>
> 1 tablespoon all-purpose flour
>
> 2 to 3 cups chicken broth
>
> 1 cup chopped green New Mexico chile, roasted, peeled, stems removed
>
> 1 small tomato, peeled and chopped

In a medium skillet, heat the oil and saute the onion and garlic until they are soft. Stir in the flour and blend well. Simmer for a couple of minutes to cook the flour, being careful it does not brown. Slowly add the broth, and stir until smooth.

Stir in the remaining ingredients and bring to a boil, then reduce the heat and simmer until the sauce has thickened, about fifteen minutes.

Yield: 2 to 3 cups **Heat scale:** Medium

Dave's Fresh Red Chile Sauce

This method of making chile sauce differs from others using fresh New Mexican chiles because the chiles aren't roasted and peeled first. Because of the high sugar content of fresh red chiles, this sauce is sweeter than most. Dave harvested some chiles from his garden one late summer day, made a batch of this sauce, and ate every drop as a soup! It makes a tasty enchilada sauce, too.

> 1/4 cup vegetable oil
>
> 8 fresh red New Mexican chiles, seeds and stems
>   removed, chopped (or more, to taste)
>
> 1 large onion, chopped
>
> 3 cloves garlic
>
> 4 cups water
>
> 1/4 teaspoon ground cumin
>
> 1 tablespoon minced fresh cilantro
>
> 1/2 teaspoon Mexican oregano leaves
>
> Salt to taste

Heat the oil in a large saucepan, and saute the chiles, onion, and garlic until the onion is soft, about seven minutes.

Add the remaining ingredients and bring to a boil, then reduce the heat and simmer uncovered for one hour. In a blender, puree the sauce in batches and return it to the saucepan.

Cook until the sauce thickens to the desired consistency. Add salt to taste.

Yield: About 3 cups   **Heat scale:** Mild to medium

Classic New Mexican Red Chile Sauce

This basic sauce can be used in any recipe calling for a red sauce, either traditional Mexican or new Southwestern versions of beans, tacos, tamales, and enchiladas.

> 10 to 12 dried, whole, red New Mexican chiles
> 1 large onion, chopped
> 3 cloves garlic, chopped
> 3 cups water

Place the chiles on a baking pan, and put them in a 250-degree oven for about ten to fifteen minutes, or until the chiles smell like they are toasted, taking care not to let them burn. Remove the stems and seeds, and crumble the pods into a saucepan.

Add the remaining ingredients, bring to a boil, reduce the heat, and simmer for twenty to thirty minutes.

Puree the mixture in a blender until smooth, and strain if necessary. If the sauce is too thin, place it back on the stove and simmer until it is reduced to the desired consistency.

Variations: Spices such as cumin, coriander, and Mexican oregano may be added to taste.

Yield: 2 to 2½ cups   **Heat scale:** Medium

Salsa *Fresca* with Green Chile

This universal salsa, also known as *salsa fria, salsa cruda, pico de gallo, salsa Mexicana,* and *salsa picante,* is served all over the Southwest, and often shows up with nontraditional ingredients such as canned tomatoes, bell peppers, or spices like oregano. Here is the most authentic version. Remember that all the ingredients should be as fresh as possible, and the vegetables must be hand-chopped. Never, never use a blender or food processor. Pico de gallo ("rooster's beak," for its sharpness) is best when the tomatoes come from the garden rather than the supermarket. It can be used as a dip for chips or for spicing up fajitas and other Southwestern specialties. (Note: This recipe requires advance preparation, and will keep for only a day or two in the refrigerator.)

> 1 cup chopped New Mexico green chiles, roasted,
>   peeled, seeds and stems removed
> 2 large, ripe tomatoes, finely chopped
> 1 medium onion, peeled and chopped fine
> 1/4 cup minced fresh cilantro
> 2 tablespoons vinegar
> 2 tablespoons vegetable oil

Combine all the ingredients in a large bowl, mix well, and let the salsa sit, covered, for at least an hour to blend the flavors.

Yield: 3 cups   **Heat scale:** Medium

SOUTHWEST SEASONING RUB

This a l-purpose rub adds a taste of the Southwest to whatever you use it on. It's a great grill rub for chicken, beef, or pork. It adds another chile dimension to salsas, and the chipotle's hint of smoke complements a pot of pinto beans.

> 2 tablespoons ground red New Mexico chile,
>   such as Chimayó
> 2 teaspoons ground chile de arbol
> 1 teaspoon ground chipotle chile
> 2 teaspoons ground cumin
> 1 teaspoon freshly ground black pepper
> 1 teaspoon garlic salt
> 1 teaspoon salt

Combine all the ingredients in a bowl, and stir to blend. Store the mixture in an airtight container.

Yield: 1/3 cup **Heat scale:** Medium

Appetizers
and
Breakfast

The Ultimate Chilehead Guacamole

This pulpy sauce moved from strictly Mexican use into America around 1900 and slowly increased in popularity as the avocado became more available in American supermarkets. It really took off after the introduction of corn chips in the 1960s, and now is found premade in various packages everywhere. But many of these are bland and lack the full flavor of guacamole made from scratch. This version is traditionally made with a *molcajete y mano,* a large Mexican mortar and pestle carved from volcanic rock. If you don't have a *molcajete y mano,* you can smash the avocados with a fork or potato masher.

2 ripe avocados

1/2 tomato, chopped

1/2 clove garlic

1/2 cup chopped New Mexican chiles, roasted,
    peeled, seeds and stems removed, chopped

1 tablespoon chopped cilantro

2 limes

Salt to taste

For the Chips:

12 small, fresh corn tortillas, cut into wedges

2 cups corn oil

Salt to taste

Peel and pit the avocados, then grind them in the molcajete. Add the tomato, garlic, chiles, and cilantro, and keep

(continued on next page)

grinding. Gently squeeze in the lime juice, and add salt to taste. Transfer to a bowl, and serve with fresh Mexican tortilla chips.

To make the chips, heat the oil in a large frying pan until it reaches 350 degrees. Fry the tortilla wedges in batches, cooking each for about three minutes or until it becomes a nice shade of golden brown. Drain the chips on a paper towel, sprinkle them with salt, and keep warm in a 200-degree oven.

Yield: 4 to 6 servings **Heat scale:** Medium

Disappearing Chile Strips

As the title of this recipe suggests, these marinated chile strips won't last long around a hot and spicy house. Extremely versatile, they can be rolled up and pegged with a toothpick for an appetizer, jazz up a favorite sandwich (I like them with grilled cheese), be coarsely chopped for your favorite pasta salad, or added to spice up an omelette or frittata.

> 1 pound fresh green New Mexican chiles (or frozen whole pods that you defrost), roasted, peeled, seeds and stems removed, and cut into 1/4-inch-wide strips
> 1/4 cup olive oil
> 1/4 cup red wine vinegar
> 1 clove of garlic, minced

Place the chile strips in a ceramic casserole dish, and cover with the remaining ingredients. Stir the mixture very gently to coat the chile. Marinate overnight in the refrigerator.

Yield: $1^1/_2$ cups **Heat scale:** Mild to medium

Sweet Potato Chips Dusted with Chimayó Red Chile

This appetizer is a hot twist on party chips. I have had great success substituting sweet potatoes for potatoes in many dishes.

> 2 large sweet potatoes, peeled and cut into
> 1/4 inch wafers
> Vegetable oil for deep frying
> 1 tablespoon New Mexican hot red chile powder
> (Chimayó preferred)

Heat the vegetable oil to 350 degrees in a deep skillet. Separate the potatoes into six portions. Fry each batch, turning once, for one minute or until they are golden. With a slotted spoon, transfer the chips to a paper towel to drain and cool. Continue until all the potato chips are fried and cooled.

Place the red chile powder in a medium-sized plastic bag. Again working in batches, place the chips in the bag and close it. Shake the bag gently to dust the chips with the powder. After each batch is dusted, transfer to a napkin-lined basket and serve.

Yield: 4 to 6 servings **Heat scale:** Medium

HOT SHOT OLIVES

These olives, which keep for several months in the refrigerator, can be used as an appetizer or for a spicy addition to salads. Try them chopped and mixed with cream cheese and a little mayonnaise as a tangy stuffing for celery or hard-boiled eggs. You can also incorporate them (chopped or sliced) into any dipping recipe to liven it up. Note: This recipe requires advance preparation.

> 1¼ pounds Kalamata olives
> 3 garlic cloves, thinly sliced
> 1½ teaspoons rosemary, crushed with a
>   mortar and pestle
> 1 tablespoon New Mexican red chile molido or
>   pure red ground chile
> 2 tablespoons balsamic vinegar
> 1½ cups olive oil

Drain the olives thoroughly, and set aside. Mix the remaining ingredients together, and whisk thoroughly.

In a one-quart jar, place one-third of the olives and cover with one-third of the whisked mixture; repeat with the next third of the olives and the mixture, until both are used up.

Let the olives stand at room temperature for twenty-four hours. Then shake the jar well, and place it in the refrigerator for two weeks, shaking the jar daily.

Yield: 3 cups of olives   **Heat scale:** Mild

Huevos Rancheros de Nuevo Mexico (New Mexican Ranch-Style Eggs)

The recipes may vary from place to place in Mexico and the Southwest, but the bottom line with ranch-style eggs is that they are spicy and delicious for a hearty breakfast or a brunch served with refried beans and hash-brown potatoes.

> **2 cups Green Chile Sauce (recipe on page 29)**
> **8 eggs**
> **4 corn tortillas**
> **Vegetable oil for frying**
> **1 medium tomato, chopped, for garnish**
> **1/2 cup grated cheddar**

Heat the chile sauce in a frying pan.

Crack the eggs into the sauce, cover the pan with a lid, and poach the eggs to the desired consistency.

Heat two inches of vegetable oil in a saute pan. Fry each tortilla in the oil for a few seconds on each side until soft, then remove and drain on paper towels.

To serve, slip the eggs with the sauce onto the tortillas, add the grated cheddar, garnish with the tomatoes, and serve.

Yield: 4 servings **Heat scale:** Medium

Southwest Breakfast Burritos

This all-purpose filling is used here to make a breakfast meal wrapped in a warm flour tortilla, but it is also great in taco shells. In fact, the eggs taste great all by themselves.

8 ounces chorizo

1/2 cup chopped onion

1 clove garlic, peeled and chopped

6 eggs, beaten

1 tablespoon crushed, dried, red New Mexican chile

1/4 teaspoon ground cumin

1 cup grated cheddar or Monterey Jack cheese

1 small tomato, cored and diced

1 small avocado, peeled, pitted, and diced

4 flour tortillas

Chopped fresh cilantro for garnish

In a skillet over medium heat, cook the chorizo, stirring occasionally to break up any clumps. Drain it on a paper towel, pour off all but two teaspoons of the accumulated oil, and return the pan to medium heat.

Add the onion and garlic to the pan, and saute until they are soft, about five minutes. Stir in the eggs, chile, and cumin. Scramble until the eggs are firm and cooked through. Remove the pan from the heat, and stir in the cheese, tomato, and avocado.

Divide the eggs evenly among the four tortillas, and top the filling with the cilantro. Roll the tortillas burrito-style and serve.

Yield: 4 servings **Heat scale:** Medium

Soups and
Salads

Sopa de Lima

This light, delicate soup is easy to prepare and makes a great beginning for either lunch or dinner. Freely translated as "lime soup," it's made in Mexico with sour lemons which are unavailable in this country, but limes make a suitable substitute.

> 1 green New Mexican chile, roasted, peeled,
>   seeds and stem removed, chopped
> 1/3 cup onions, chopped
> 2 teaspoons vegetable oil
> 4 cups chicken broth
> 1 cup cooked shredded chicken
> Salt to taste
> 1 tomato, peeled and chopped
> Juice of 1 lime
> 4 large lime slices for garnish
> Tortilla chips for garnish

Saute the chile and onion in the oil until the onion is soft but not browned. Add the chicken broth, chicken, and salt to taste, cover, and simmer twenty minutes. Add the tomato, and simmer five minutes longer. Stir in the lime juice, taste, and add more if needed.

Serve in bowls garnished with a lime slice and a couple of tortilla chips.

Yield: 4 servings   **Heat scale:** Mild

Green Chile Stew

I couldn't put together a collection of New Mexican chile recipes without including my favorite—green chile stew. This has been a popular staple in northern New Mexico for hundreds of years, ever since the Spanish introduced domesticated pigs. In the late summer and early fall, when the crops come in and everyone starts roasting and putting up chiles for the coming year, I keep a pot of this stew simmering on the stove to fill containers for freezing to enjoy during the cold winter months.

1½ pounds lean pork, cut into 1 1/2-inch cubes
Vegetable oil
1 large onion, diced
2 garlic cloves, minced
1 quart pork or chicken broth
6 to 8 green New Mexico chiles, roasted, peeled,
    and cut into thin strips
2 small tomatoes, peeled and chopped
1 large potato, peeled and diced
1/2 teaspoon dried oregano, Mexican preferred
Salt to taste

In a heavy skillet, brown the pork over medium to medium-high heat, adding a little oil if needed. Then transfer it to a large stockpot. Add the onions and some more oil to the skillet, and cook until the onions turn a golden brown, five to ten minutes. Add the garlic, and cook for an additional minute. Transfer the mixture to the pot with the pork.

Add two cups of broth to the skillet, raise the heat, and deglaze the skillet, being sure to scrape all the bits and pieces from the sides and bottom. Pour the broth over the pork in the stockpot.

Add the remaining ingredients to the stockpot, bring it to just below boiling, reduce the heat, and simmer for an hour to an hour and a half, or until the meat is very tender and starts to fall apart.

Yield: 4 servings **Heat scale:** Medium

Posole with Chile Caribe

One of my favorite restaurants in Albuquerque, El Patio, provided this recipe, which is the classic version prepared in northern New Mexico. Serving the chile caribe as a side dish instead of mixing it with the posole lets guests adjust the heat to their own liking. Note: This variation requires advance preparation.

Posole:

2 dried red New Mexican chiles, stems and seeds removed

8 ounces frozen posole corn or dry posole corn that
  has been soaked in water overnight

1 teaspoon garlic powder

1 medium onion, chopped

6 cups water

1 pound pork loin, cut in 1-inch cubes

Chopped fresh cilantro for garnish

Chopped onion for garnish

Combine all the ingredients in a pot except the pork, and boil at medium heat for about three hours or until the posole is tender, adding more water if necessary.

Add the pork, and continue cooking for half an hour, or until the pork is tender but not falling apart. The result should resemble a soup more than a stew. Remove the chile pods before serving.

Chile Caribe:

6 dried red New Mexican chiles, stems and
   seeds removed
1 quart water
1 teaspoon garlic powder

Simmer the chile pods in the water for fifteen minutes. Remove the pods, combine with the garlic powder, and puree in a blender, using a little chile water to thin if necessary. Transfer to a serving bowl, and allow to cool.

The posole is served in soup bowls accompanied by warm flour tortillas. Three additional bowls of garnishes should be provided: the chile caribe, chopped cilantro, and chopped onion. Each guest can then adjust the pungency of the posole according to individual taste.

Variation: For really hot chile caribe, add dried red chile piquins, cayenne chiles, or chiles de arbol to the New Mexicans.

Yield: 4 servings **Heat scale:** Medium but varies according to the amount of chile added

Chile con Carne with Frozen Red or Green Chile

Here is a classic recipe from my good friend Nancy Gerlach, who commented: "When you order 'chile con carne' in New Mexico, this is what you will be served. It is a basic recipe that has its roots in very old Pueblo Indian cooking. Beef can be substituted in this recipe."

> 2 pounds pork, cut into 3/4-inch cubes
> 2 tablespoons vegetable oil
> 3 cloves garlic, minced
> 2 cups frozen New Mexican chile, red or green, thawed
> 3 cups water or beef broth
> Salt to taste

Brown the pork in the oil in a Dutch oven. Add the garlic, and saute. Pour off any excess fat.

Add the chile, pork, and water; bring to a boil, reduce the heat, and simmer covered until the pork is very tender and starts to fall apart, at least two hours.

Yield: 6 to 8 servings **Heat scale:** Medium

Jicama and Orange Salad

Jicama is a Mexican root vegetable whose taste and consistency is a combination of a water chestnut, an apple, and a potato. In fact, some cooks substitute jicama for water chestnuts in Asian recipes. It can be combined with any number of fruits and vegetables because it blends so well with so many flavors.

1 head Romaine lettuce, cleaned and dried
1/2 pound jicama, peeled and sliced paper thin
6 seedless oranges, peeled and sectioned
2 red onions, sliced
2 teaspoons ground New Mexican red chile powder
1/2 cup olive oil
6 tablespoons fresh lime juice
3 tablespoons red wine vinegar
3 tablespoons orange marmalade
Freshly ground black pepper

Line a shallow bowl with the Romaine leaves. Alternate overlapping circles of jicama, oranges, and onion rings on the leaves.

Combine the remaining ingredients in a small glass jar, and shake well. Pour the dressing over the salad, and serve immediately.

Yield: 4 to 6 servings   **Heat scale:** Medium

Green Chile Panzanella (Southwest-Style Tuscan Bread Salad)

In this recipe, it is very important to use the best quality red wine vinegar and olive oil because even the heat of the green chile will not mask the biting taste of inferior products. This salad is surprisingly refreshing on a hot day because of the vinegar and the fresh vegetables. It is also a great way to use up leftover bread—but once again, it has to be bread with substance. Soft, squishy, store-bought, plastic-wrapped bread will make a salad akin to Elmer's Glue!

> 10 slices of good quality, coarse-grained bread,
>   several days old
> Water to soak the bread
> 3 very fresh tomatoes, peeled and coarsely chopped
> 2 cucumbers, peeled, seeded, and cubed
> 1 cup finely diced red onion
> 2 cloves garlic, minced very fine
> 1 cup chopped New Mexican green chile
> 1/2 cup fresh basil, chopped
> 1/4 cup red wine vinegar
> 1/4 teaspoon salt
> 1/4 teaspoon freshly ground black pepper
> 2/3 cup best olive oil

In a large bowl, soak the bread with a little water, but don't make it totally soggy. Squeeze the bread dry with your hands, and crumble it into a large bowl. Add the tomatoes, cucumbers, red onion, garlic, chile, and basil, and toss with the bread.

Pour the vinegar into a small glass jar, and add the salt and pepper. Shake it until the salt is dissolved. Then add the olive oil, and shake until the mixture is blended.

Immediately pour the vinegar and oil mixture over the bread mixture, and toss gently. Serve immediately.

Yield: 5 servings **Heat scale:** Medium

Succulent Southwest Potato Salad

Here is my favorite spicy potato salad. It calls for chile powder and sauce instead of pods to elevate the heat level.

> 4 medium Russet potatoes
>
> 1/4 cup olive oil
>
> 1/4 cup white wine vinegar
>
> 2½ teaspoons red New Mexican chile powder
>
> 1 teaspoon bottled hot sauce
>
> 1/2 cup chopped onion
>
> 1 can whole kernel corn, drained and rinsed
>   (8 ounces)
>
> 1/2 cup coarsely shredded carrot
>
> 1/3 cup chopped green bell pepper
>
> 1/2 cup sliced ripe olives

Place the potatoes in a Dutch oven, and cover with water. Bring the water to a boil, then turn the heat down to a gentle boil. Cook for fifteen to twenty minutes, or until a knife pierces the potatoes easily. Drain, peel, and cube them into a large bowl while still warm.

In a small glass jar, combine the oil, vinegar, chile powder, and hot sauce, and shake vigorously. Pour over the potatoes, and toss gently. Add the remaining ingredients, and toss gently again.

Refrigerate for one hour before serving.

Yield: 4 to 6 servings **Heat scale:** Medium

Main
Dishes

Grilled Piñon Lamb Chops

Here is a delicious combination of ingredients from the Southwest—pine nuts, chile, and lamb. For an authentic, smoky flavor, grill them over mesquite wood or charcoal covered with mesquite chips soaked in water.

> 1 tablespoon ground red New Mexican chile
>
> 3/4 cup olive oil
>
> 5 tablespoons roasted piñons or pine nuts
>
> 1/2 cup tomato paste
>
> 1/4 cup vinegar
>
> 3 cloves garlic
>
> 4 lamb chops, cut 1 to 1½ inches thick

Combine all the ingredients except the lamb in a blender, and puree until smooth. Paint the chops with the mixture, and let them marinate for at least an hour.

Grill the chops, turning occasionally until done, about seven to ten minutes a side.

Yield: 4 servings **Heat scale:** Mild

Perfect Santa Fe Enchiladas

Cooking perfect Santa Fe enchiladas from scratch is a bit of an ordeal but well worth the time and trouble. If you have extra machaca and sauce, they both freeze well. Serve with refried beans. In northern New Mexico, home-fried potatoes are also served.

Machaca Shredded Beef:
3-pound arm roast

Water

1½ cups coarsely chopped green chile

1 tomato, chopped

1/2 onion, diced

1/2 teaspoon garlic powder

Red Chile Sauce:See recipe on page 36 or page 37.

The Enchiladas:
12 blue corn tortillas

Vegetable oil

Machaca beef

1 large onion, finely chopped

3 cups shredded cheddar cheese

Shredded lettuce for garnish

Finely chopped tomatoes for garnish

To make the machaca, place the roast in a large pan with water to cover, and simmer until tender and the meat begins to fall apart, about three to four hours. Remove the roast from the pan, remove the fat and bone, and shred the meat by hand or with a fork.

Return the meat to the pan, add the remaining ingredients, stir well, and simmer until all the liquid has been absorbed by the meat, about thirty minutes.

To make the enchiladas, place a little oil in a small skillet, and heat until almost smoking. Using tongs, fry each tortilla in the oil for about five seconds a side, turning once. Do not overcook, or the tortillas will be tough. Drain them on paper towels. Add oil as needed when frying the tortillas.

To assemble the enchiladas, place a single tortilla on an oven-proof plate. Spread about 1/4 cup of machaca beef over the tortilla, and sprinkle on some onion and cheese. Spread about 3 tablespoons of chile sauce over the cheese. Place a second tortilla over the first, pour about 3/4 cup chile sauce over it, and top with about 1/2 cup of cheese. Repeat with the remaining five plates.

Then place them in a 350-degree oven for about twenty minutes. Remove, and garnish with the lettuce and tomatoes.

Yield: 6 servings   Heat scale: Medium

New Mexico Carne Adovada

This variation of an ancient recipe evolved from the need to preserve meat before refrigeration. The red chile acts as an antioxidant, and prevents the meat from spoiling. But such technical details should not detract from the fact that this simple dish is incredibly tasty, and once eaten, is never forgotten. Note: This recipe requires advance preparation.

1½ cups crushed red New Mexican chiles, stems removed, seeds included

4 cloves garlic, minced

1 teaspoon dried oregano

3 cups water

2 pounds pork, cut into strips

2 medium potatoes, peeled and chopped

2 onions, chopped

Combine chile, garlic, and oregano in a sauce pan. Add the water, and heat for five minutes to make a coarse chile sauce.

Place the pork in a glass pan, and cover with the chile sauce. Marinate the pork for twelve to twenty-four hours in the refrigerator, turning once or twice.

Add the potatoes and onions to the pork and chile, and bake in a 300-degree oven for two hours or until the pork is very tender and starts to fall apart.

Serving suggestions: Place the adovada mixture in a flour tortilla, top with grated cheese, and eat as a burrito. Or use it as a stuffing for sopaipillas or a filling for enchiladas.

Yield: 6 servings **Heat scale:** Hot

Roulade of Pork with Green Chile and Cilantro

This simple-to-prepare pork roast makes a dramatic presentation when it is carved at the table. Serve it with applesauce, sour cream whipped potatoes, and a vegetable of your choice.

> 3 cups chopped green New Mexican chile, roasted,
>   peeled, stems removed
> 1 medium onion, chopped
> 6 cloves garlic, chopped
> 1 small Granny Smith apple, cored and chopped
> 1/2 cup chopped fresh cilantro
> 3 tablespoons butter or margarine
> 3-pound pork roast, boned
> Flour for dredging
> 2 cups white wine
> 2 tablespoons flour mixed with 1/4 cup water

Preheat the oven to 450 degrees.

Saute the onions, garlic, and apple in the butter until soft. Add the chile and cilantro. Spread the mixture on the pork, roll it up, and tie the roast in four to six places to hold it together. Lightly dust the pork with flour.

Place the pork on a rack in a roasting pan, reduce the heat to 350 degrees, and roast uncovered until done, usually thirty-five minutes per pound. The internal temperature should be 185 degrees.

Remove the pork, and keep warm. Deglaze the pan with

(continued on next page)

wine, and strain the drippings. Place the strained wine in a saucepan, bring to a boil, and slowly pour the flour mixture into the drippings to thicken and form a glaze. Add more wine to thin if necessary.

Carve the pork, and serve with the wine sauce on the side.

Yield: 6 servings   **Heat scale:** Mild

Stuffed Chicken Breasts with Walnut *Pipián* Sauce

The Mayans are credited with creating "pipián," or sauces that are both flavored and thickened with seeds and/or nuts. In this recipe, the pipián also adds color to the dish.

3 chicken breasts, skinned, bone removed, cut in half

6 green New Mexican chiles, roasted, peeled, stems and seeds removed, left whole

6 thin slices ham

6 slices asadaro or Monterey Jack cheese

1 large avocado, peeled and sliced

3 tablespoons chopped fresh cilantro

1/4 cup melted margarine

1 medium onion, chopped

1 clove garlic, chopped

1 poblano, roasted, peeled, stem and seeds removed, chopped

4 tablespoons margarine or vegetable oil

1/2 cup chopped walnuts

1/4 cup freshly chopped cilantro

2 cups chicken broth

Pound the chicken breasts until thin. Top each piece with the chile, ham, cheese, avocado, and cilantro, then roll it tightly, place fold down, and brush with the margarine. Cover, and bake for forty-five minutes at 325 degrees. Remove the cover, and continue to bake until the top is golden brown.

(continued on next page)

To make the sauce, saute the onion, garlic, and chile in the oil until the onion starts to brown. Place the mixture and the walnuts in a blender, and puree until smooth, using a little broth to thin if necessary.

Return it to the saucepan, stir in the broth, and simmer for twenty to thirty minutes until thickened.

To serve, place the chicken on a plate, pour the sauce over the top, and garnish with a few chopped walnut pieces.

Yield: 4 to 6 servings   **Heat scale:** Mild

Tamale Pie with Cheese and Chicken

This recipe is a delicious alternative to traditional tamales.
A green salad is all that is needed to complete a meal.

> 1 chicken (4 pounds), cut in pieces
> 2 large onions, chopped
> 2 cloves garlic, minced
> 4 green New Mexican chiles, roasted, peeled, stems
>   and seeds removed, chopped
> 3 jalapeño chiles, stems removed, chopped
> 1 teaspoon New Mexican red chile powder
> 1 cup ripe olives, chopped
> 1 cup whole kernel corn
> 2 cups sour cream
> 2 cups chicken broth
> 1 cup masa harina
> 2 eggs, separated
> 2 cups grated Monterey Jack cheese

Simmer the chicken, half of the onions, and the garlic in water to cover until the chicken is done and starts to fall away from the bones. Remove the chicken. Strain the broth and reserve.

Remove the meat from the bones, and chop the chicken along with the remaining onion. Combine with the chiles, chile powder, olives, corn, and sour cream. Place the mixture in a casserole dish.

Bring the broth to a boil, and gradually add the masa

(continued on next page)

while stirring constantly. Reduce the heat, and cook until the mixture thickens, about ten minutes. Remove from the heat, and stir in the egg yolks. Whip the egg whites until stiff, and fold them into the masa mixture. Spread this batter over the casserole, and top with the grated cheese.

Bake for thirty-five minutes at 375 degrees.

Yield: 6 servings   **Heat scale:** Medium

Side
Dishes

Calabacitas con Chiles Verdes (Squash and Green Chile)

Squash and corn are familiar accompaniments throughout the Southwest. This recipe is particularly good with traditional entrees such as enchiladas, tamales, and burritos.

    1 cup chopped onions
    2 cloves garlic, minced
    1 tablespoon bacon drippings or vegetable oil
    4 green New Mexican chiles, roasted, peeled, stems
        and seeds removed, chopped
    2 medium zucchini, sliced
    1 cup whole kernel corn
    1/3 cup cream or half-and-half

Saute the onions and garlic in the drippings until soft.

Add the chiles, zucchini, and corn. Simmer for fifteen to twenty minutes or until the squash is almost done.

Add the cream, increase the heat until it starts to boil, and cook until the vegetables are done and the sauce has thickened.

Yield: 6 servings **Heat scale:** Medium

Chiles Rellenos

Chiles rellenos literally means "stuffed chiles," and in Mexico, many different chiles are used, including poblanos, jalapeños, rocotos, and even fresh pasillas. Here in the Southwest, we prefer New Mexican green chiles. Whatever type of chile you use, the preparation and fillings are the same.

 1 medium onion, chopped
 2 cloves garlic, minced
 2 tablespoons butter or margarine
 2½ cups cooked whole kernel corn
 1 teaspoon dried oregano
 1/3 cup sour cream
 6 ounces cheddar cheese, cubed
 6 green New Mexican chiles, roasted and peeled,
  stems left on
 Flour for dredging
 3 eggs, separated
 3 tablespoons flour
 1 tablespoon water
 1/4 teaspoon salt
 Vegetable oil
 Green Chile Sauce (recipe on page 29)

Saute the onion and garlic in the butter until soft. Add the corn and oregano, and cook for an additional five minutes. Remove from the heat, and stir in the sour cream and cheese. Make a slit in the side of each chile, and stuff with the corn
(continued on next page)

mixture. Dredge the chiles in the flour, and shake off any excess.

Beat the egg whites until they form stiff peaks. Then beat the yolks with the water, the tablespoon of flour, and the salt. Fold the yolks into the whites.

Dip the chiles in the egg batter, and fry in one to two inches of oil until they are golden brown. Serve topped with the green chile sauce.

Yield: 6 servings   **Heat scale:** Mild

Papas con Chile Colorado (Potatoes with Red Chile)

Although the word *COLORADO* here refers to the red color of the chile rather than the state of the same name, this dish is commonly prepared there—and all over the Southwest. Serve these red chile potatoes in place of hash browns for a terrific Southwestern breakfast.

> 2 tablespoons butter
> 1/2 cup chopped onions
> 1 clove garlic minced
> 2 tablespoons crushed red New Mexican chile,
>   including the seeds
> 2 large potatoes, peeled and diced
> 1 tablespoon grated Parmesan cheese

Saute the onions and garlic in the butter until soft, then add the chile. Toss the potatoes in the mixture.

Place the potatoes on a shallow pan with a little water, and bake in a 350-degree oven until the potatoes are done, about forty-five minutes.

Sprinkle the cheese over the top of the potatoes, and serve.

Yield: 4 servings **Heat scale:** Medium

A Drink
and
A Dessert

BLOODY MARIA

Think this drink is just a bloody mary with tequila switched for the vodka? Well, almost.

> 2 ounces tequila
>
> 3 ounces tomato juice
>
> 1/4 ounce lime juice
>
> Dash Worcestershire sauce
>
> Dash celery salt
>
> Dash black pepper
>
> Dash salt
>
> 1 teaspoon New Mexico red chile powder

Combine all ingredients in a small pitcher, and pour over ice in a glass. Garnish with a slice of lime, and serve.

Yield: 1 serving   **Heat scale:** Medium

THE HONORABLE *BISCOCHITO* FROM THE LAND OF ENCHANTMENT

These cookies are so distinctly New Mexican that, despite the fact that they were copied directly from Old Mexican *BIZCOCHITOS*, they were named the New Mexico State Cookie in 1989. By the way, they are at their delicious best when spiced up just a little with native New Mexican Chimayó chile powder. You can buy cookie cutters in Southwestern shapes online.

    1 pound soft butter
    1½ cups sugar
    2 teaspoons anise seeds
    2 eggs, beaten
    6 cups flour
    3 teaspoons baking powder
    1 teaspoon salt
    1/2 cup brandy
    1/4 cup sugar
    1 tablespoon ground cinnamon
    1 teaspoon Chimayó chile powder

Cream together the butter, sugar, and anise seeds in a bowl. Add the eggs, and beat well.

Mix the flour, baking powder, and salt, and sift together three times into another bowl.

Add the flour mixture one cup at a time to the creamed butter, mixing well after each addition, until all the flour is used.

Pour the brandy over the dough, and mix well. Lightly knead the dough to hold it together.

Combine the sugar, cinnamon, and chile powder in a separate bowl. Roll out the dough to 1/4-inch thickness, and cut into fancy shapes, such as chiles, coyotes, or saguaro cacti (even if they don't grow in New Mexico).

Dip each cookie in the cinnamon sugar, and then bake on a cookie sheet at 350 degrees for ten to twelve minutes or until golden brown.

Yield: 4 to 5 dozen **Heat scale:** Mild

PART 4
Resources

FURTHER READING

- DeWitt, Dave and Paul W. Bosland. *The Complete Chile Pepper Book: Choosing, Growing, Preserving, and Cooking.* Portland, OR: Timber Press, 2009.
- DeWitt, Dave. *1001 Best Hot & Spicy Recipes.* Chicago: Surrey Books, 2010.
- DeWitt, Dave. *The Southwest Table: Traditional Foods from Texas, New Mexico, and Arizona.* New York: Lyons Press, 2011.
- DeWitt, Dave. *Dave DeWitt's Chile Trivia.* Albuquerque: Sunbelt Media, 2012.

SEED AND PLANT SOURCES

For seeds, go to the Chile Pepper Institute, **www.chilepepperinstitute.org**, Paul W. Bosland, publisher; Danise Coon, editor.

For five hundred varieties of chile pepper bedding plants in season and fresh chile pods in the late summer and early fall, go to Cross Country Nurseries, **www.chileplants.com**, Janie Lamson, publisher.

WEBSITES

For detailed information on chile peppers around the world:

- The Fiery Foods and Barbecue SuperSite, **www.fieryfoods.com**, Dave DeWitt, publisher; Lois Manno, editor. This site has more than four hundred articles on chile varieties, gardening, history, cooking, and Q&As.

• The Chileman, **www.thechileman.org**, Mark McMillan, publisher and editor. This U.K. site contains the best glossary of chile pepper varieties, with about four thousand listed.

• Pepperworld.com, **www.pepperworld.com** (German language), Harald Zoschke, publisher and editor. The site's many articles include European chile-growing information.

• The Chile Pepper Institute, **www.chilepepperinstitute.org**, Paul W. Bosland, publisher and director; Danise Coon, editor and assistant director. The shop at this site contains books, chile information, and the seeds for dozens of chile varieties.

• Fatalii.net, **www.fatalii.net**, a Finnish site, in English, with extensive information about chile growing and bonsai chiles. Jukka Kilpinnen is the publisher and editor.

• The Burn! Blog, **www.burn-blog.com**, which keeps chile-heads and BBQ freaks in touch with the latest news, personalities, and weirdness in the worlds of chile peppers, spiced-up foods, and barbecues

CHILE PEPPER SUPPLIERS AND ONLINE HOTSHOPS

MexGrocer, **www.MexGrocer.com**, has many varieties of worldwide chiles as dried pods and powders.

Melissa's/World Variety Produce, Inc., **www.melissas.com**, has worldwide fresh chiles in season, as well as a fine collection of dried pods and powders.

Peppers, **www.peppers.com**, has the best selection of chile pepper and barbecue products such as hot sauces, salsas, jams, cookies, candies, rubs, chili mixes—the list is very long.

If Dave DeWitt's life were a menu, it would feature dishes as diverse as alligator stew and apple pie à la mode—not to mention the beloved chile peppers that have become the basic ingredient of so many of his projects and accomplishments.

Since starting out in the electronic media, Dave has built careers as a businessman, educator, administrator, producer, on-camera personality, author, and publisher. Currently, in addition to serving as CEO of Sunbelt Shows and co-producer of the National Fiery Foods & Barbecue Show, Dave is always busy sharing his chile pepper expertise in as wide a range of forums as possible.

Besides writing more than forty books (mostly on fiery foods but also including novels, food histories, and travel guides), Dave is publisher of the Fiery Foods & BBQ Super Site (at **www.fiery-foods.com**), and was a founder of Chile Pepper magazine and Fiery Foods & Barbecue magazine.

From his beginning as a radio announcer, Dave went on to own audio/video production companies for which he wrote, produced, and voiced hundreds of radio and television commercials. After moving to New Mexico in 1974, he wrote and hosted the "Captain Space" TV show which beat out both "Saturday Night Live" and "Star Trek" in its Saturday midnight time slot, and, in an entirely different sphere, curated the Albuquerque Museum's 1984 exhibit *Edward S. Curtis in New Mexico*.

The interest in chile peppers and spicy foods that has helped make Dave one of the foremost authorities in the world has led to such best-sellers as *The Whole Chile Pepper Book*, *The Pepper Garden*, *The Hot Sauce Bible*, *The Chile Pepper Encyclopedia*, and *The Spicy Food Lover's Bible*. His latest book on the subject is *Chile Trivia*. As the ultimate testament to his fame and achievement, *The New York Times* has declared him to be "the Pope of Peppers."

Dave is an associate professor in Consumer and Environmental Sciences on the adjunct faculty of New Mexico State University, and also serves as chair of the Board of Regents of the New Mexico Farm and Ranch Heritage Museum.